OUR SOUTHERN NEIGHBOR MEXICO

SPORTS OF MEXICO

BY ERICA M. STOKES

A young baseball fan in Mexico holds his scorecard at a game during the mid-1940s. Mexico's official baseball teams were started over a century ago. However, baseball is just one of many sports that Mexicans enjoy today.

OUR
SOUTHERN NEIGHBOR
MEXICO

SPORTS OF MEXICO

BY ERICA M. STOKES

Mason Crest Publishers
Philadelphia

Mason Crest Publishers
370 Reed Road
Broomall PA 19008
www.masoncrest.com

3 5 7 9 8 6 4 2

Library of Congress Cataloging-in-Publication Data

Stokes, Erica M.
  Sports of Mexico/by Erica M. Stokes.
    p.   cm. — (Mexico: Our Southern Neighbor)
Includes bibliographical references and index.
Contents: Team sports are tops in Mexico—Animal sports, tradition
  or cruelty?—Mexico: where water runs high and adventure runs everywhere
  —Mexicans ride 'em, rope 'em, and wrangle 'em—Mexicans hold the ball in
  their court: handball, jai alai, and tennis—Mexicans salute solo sports.
Summary: Introduces athletic activities that are popular in Mexico, providing
  historical information, "fast facts," and basic descriptions of a wide variety
  of team and individual sports.
    ISBN 1-59084-082-8
1. Sports—Mexico—Juvenile literature. 2. Sports—Mexico—History—
Juvenile literature. [1. Sports—Mexico.] I. Title. II. Series.
GV587.S76 2002
796'.0972—dc21
                                                        2001051423

TABLE OF CONTENTS

OUR
SOUTHERN NEIGHBOR
MEXICO

Roger E. Hernández
Senior Consulting Editor

INTRODUCTION

Mexico is a country in the midst of great change. And what happens in Mexico will have an important impact on the United States, its neighbor to the north.

These changes are being put in place by President Vicente Fox, who was elected in 2000. For the previous 71 years, power had been held by presidents from one single party, known in Spanish as *Partido Revolucionario Institucional* (Institutional Revolutionary Party, or PRI). Some of those presidents have been accused of corruption. President Fox, from a different party called *Partido de Acción Nacional* (National Action Party, or PAN), says he wants to eliminate that corruption. He also wants to have a friendlier relationship with the United States, and for American businesses to increase trade with Mexico. That will create more jobs, he says, and decrease poverty—which in turn will mean fewer Mexicans will find themselves forced to emigrate in search of a better life.

But it would be wrong to think of Mexico as nothing more than a poor country. Mexico has given the world some of its greatest artists and writers. Carlos Fuentes is considered one of the greatest living novelists, and poet-essayist Octavio Paz was awarded the Nobel Prize for Literature in 1990, the most prestigious honor a writer can win. Painters such as Diego Rivera and José Clemente Orozco specialized in murals, huge paintings done on walls that tell of the history of the nation. Another famous Mexican painter, Rufino Tamayo, blended the "cubist" style of modern European painters like Picasso with native folk themes.

Tamayo's paintings in many ways symbolize what Mexico is: A blend of the culture of Europe (more specifically, its Spanish version) and the indigenous cultures that predated the arrival of Columbus.

Those cultures were thriving even 3,000 years ago, when the Olmec people built imposing monuments that survive to this day in what are now the states of Tabasco and Veracruz. Later and further to the south in the Yucatán Peninsula, the Maya civilization flourished. They constructed cities in the midst of the jungle, complete with huge temples, courts in which ball games were played, and highly accurate calendars intricately carved in stone pillars. For some mysterious reason, the Mayans abandoned most of these great centers 1,100 years ago.

The Toltecs, in central Mexico, were the next major civilization. They were followed by the Aztecs. It was the Aztecs who built the city of Tenochitlán in the middle of a lake in what is now Mexico City, with long causeways connecting it to the mainland. By the early 1500s it was one of the largest cities anywhere, with perhaps 200,000 inhabitants.

Then the Spanish came. In 1519, twenty-seven years after Columbus arrived in the Americas, Hernán Cortés landed in Yucatán with just 600 soldiers plus a few cannons and horses. They marched inland, gaining allies as they went along among indigenous peoples who resented being ruled by the Aztecs. Within two years Cortés and the Spaniards ruled Mexico. They had conquered the Aztec Empire and devastated their great capital.

It was in that destruction that modern Mexico was born. The influence of the Aztecs and other indigenous people did not disappear even though untold numbers were killed. But neither can Mexico be recognized today without the Spanish influence.

Spain ruled for three centuries. Then in 1810 Mexicans began a struggle for independence from colonial Spain, much like the United States had fought for its own independence from Great Britain. In 1821 Mexico finally became an independent nation.

The newly born republic faced many difficulties. There was much poverty, especially among descendants of indigenous peoples; most of the wealth and political power was in the hands of a small elite of Spanish ancestry. To make things worse, Mexico lost almost half of its territory to the United States in a war that lasted from 1846 to 1848. Many still resent the loss of territory, which accounts for lingering anti-American sentiments among some Mexicans. The country was later occupied by France, but under national hero Benito Juárez Mexico regained its independence in 1867.

The next turning point in Mexican history came in 1911, when a revolution meant to help the millions of Mexicans stuck in poverty began against dictator Porfirio Díaz. There was violence and fighting until 1929, when Plutarco Elías Calles founded what was to become the *Partido Revolucionario Institucional*. It brought stability as well as economic progress. Yet millions of Mexicans remained in poverty, and as time went on PRI rulers became increasingly corrupt.

It was the desire of the people of Mexico to trust someone other than the candidate of PRI that resulted in the election of Fox. And so this nation of more than 100 million, with its ancient heritage, its diverse mestizo culture, its grinding poverty, and its glorious arts, stands on the brink of a new era. Modern Mexico is seeking a place as the leader of all Latin America, an ally of the United States, and an important voice in global politics. For that to happen, Mexico must narrow the gap between the rich and poor and bring more people in the middle class. It will be interesting to watch as Fox and the Mexican people work to bring their country into the first rank of nations.

A street trader in Puebla, Mexico, offers a variety of *futbol* pennants for enthusiastic fans before the 1970 World Cup.

TEAM SPORTS ARE TOPS IN MEXICO

The favorite sport of the people of Mexico is soccer, which they call *futbol*. Children and adults play this game in different **leagues**, while professional players can participate in various competitions. The Central American Championship (CONCACAF) hosts games, the Olympics also present a challenge, and the World Cup is the field of champions. Of course, **amateurs** can play in many soccer leagues throughout Mexico. Or they can even play in the comfort of their own backyards.

The history of soccer may be traced back to the first people of Mexico. The Maya played a game that resembled modern-day soccer. Their version involved a large ball and goals. Players from both teams used their hips to move the balls and score goals. Like in today's sport, players could not use their hands to touch the ball. But after the game, the losers did not exactly shake hands with the winners. Ancient carvings indicate that games often ended in human sacrifice. A game could cost players their heads!

Mexican goalie Jorge Campos dives for the ball during a championship game in Azul stadium in Mexico City. Soccer, known as *futbol*, is one of the most popular sports in Mexico.

The modern form of soccer came from Europe. It may have been first introduced into Mexico by British miners in the 1800s, but today it is more popular in Latin America than it is in the United States. Other historians say that at the start of the 20th century, people from France and England came over and started a soccer club called Pachuca. Around 1902, this turned into an amateur league, and from this the first national league was formed in 1903. By 1927, an association devoted to *futbol* had popped up. Mexico joined the Federation Internationale de Football Association (FIFA) in 1929. A national event formed in 1932 called the Copa Mexico.

But the World Cup is the single most important event in the soccer world. This prestigious game is like American football's Super Bowl. However, this contest is only held once every four years. Mexico City hosted World Cup Finals twice, in 1970 and 1986. The Mexican stadium, an **arena** that seats 110,000 people, was first called Azteca, but it is now called Estadio

JORGE CAMPOS PLAYS THE FIELD

One of Mexico's most loved sports heroes of all time is Jorge Campos. He plays the position of goalie/forward in soccer, or *futbol*. Fans cheer for him when he plays so passionately. His bright jerseys make him easy to recognize on the field.

Campos was born on October 16, 1966, in Acapulco, Guerrero. Campos's brothers taught him to play soccer on their grandfather's ranch when he was eight. He joined his first amateur team, called Iterjerap, in 1982. While growing up he also enjoyed surfing, tennis, basketball, and baseball.

In 1988, while he was still in college, Campos began playing professionally in Mexico with the prestigious UNAM Pumas. He played for Mexico in World Cup USA in 1994 and World Cup France in 1998, and participated in the Mexican League Soccer All-Star Games in 1996 and 1997. He has been called Mexico's best goalkeeper.

Guillermo Canedo. Mexican soccer teams have made it to 11 World Cup Finals since 1930. But so far, they have never made it past quarterfinals.

Soccer is popular in Mexico because the sport can be played virtually anywhere with any equipment. A person can even play the game alone. And if a team wants to play, the pickup game allows for any number of players. Whatever is handy can be substituted for the equipment, and no special court or field must be used. Goals can be made out of anything. Even the ball doesn't have to be regulation for a friendly soccer match. A scrunched up rag and some tape can do in a pinch.

Women also play soccer in Mexico. In 1999 a Mexican team qualified for the Women's World Cup tournament for the first time. Even though the team was eliminated from the tournament without winning a game, its presence in the World Cup led to the start of a women's soccer program. One of Mexico's greatest soccer coaches, Leonardo Cuéllar, has helped the development of women' soccer in the country.

Meanwhile, America, Mexico's neighbor to the north, has loved baseball for years. But Mexicans also enjoy baseball—or *beisbol*, as they call it. The people of the Yucatán peninsula, called Yucateros, really like the sport. They call baseball *"el rey de los deportes"*—the king of sports.

Some say baseball may even have first originated in Mexico. Certainly, Yucatán was one of several regions where the game was first played in the early 1890s, but most historians think that Cubans were responsible for bringing baseball to

The first great baseball player to come from Mexico was a man named Bobby Avila. In the 1950s, he played for the Cleveland Indians. Later he took up politics in Mexico.

Soccer players scatter on the field of the Azteca stadium in Mexico. Soccer is believed to have originated in Mexico, as the Mayans were known to have played a game with similar rules.

Mexico. During the Spanish American war, islanders left Cuba to get away from the fighting. Baseball was already a favorite sport on Cuba, and when they came to Mexico, they kept playing.

In Mexico, the new game soon caught on. Young men and boys began playing baseball in streets and alleyways. These games were not formal, of course. In fact, most players didn't even wear shoes. Pitchers wore no gloves. Players made bats out of sticks, boards, and pipes. Wadded up rags could be used as balls. Bases could be anything that marked a place. **Umpires** rarely wore masks.

Merida's and Progreso's real baseball teams were formed in 1892. Later, baseball parks were built. Men from wealthy families learned how to play baseball abroad, and when these men came back to Mexico, they played in the team called the Sporting Club. Baseball grew more popular, but when the economy slumped in the late 1890s, baseball's growth came to a stop.

But things picked up in again with the turn of the century. Villages set up clubs for people to play baseball. Players paid dues so they could use equipment. Wealthy men who could afford regulation gloves, bats, and balls could play in two elite teams: El Trovador, which began in 1901, and the Pablo Gonzalez Baseball Club. You didn't have to be a member of the wealthy upper class to play baseball, however; men who worked for a living could also play on the El Fenix, Railway, and Club Colon teams. Financial problems again stopped baseball's growth in 1905.

Interest in baseball did not spread throughout Mexico until the 1920s, after the Revolution. Men of different backgrounds now played in towns and villages. And this time, baseball had come to stay.

Informal baseball games in village plazas are common in Mexico. Baseball and soccer both owe their popularity in part to the fact that each sport can be played nearly anywhere, and require very little equipment.

In 1925, the Mexican League was formed. In 15 years this league became the major professional league for baseball in Mexico. In 1946 Jorge Pasquel, the commissioner of the Mexican League, even started inviting players from the United States to come and play ball for his teams.

Today, **scouts** from the United States come and **recruit** big leaguers for the major leagues. During the 1980s and 1990s, some of baseball's biggest stars, like pitcher Fernando Valenzuela and first baseman Keith Hernandez, were from Mexico. Other famous Mexican players include All-Star shortstop Nomar Garciaparra, pitcher Ismael Valdes, and outfielder Vinny Castilla.

Mexicans still like playing and watching baseball. Kids can play in little league games, while adults can play on teams. Entrance to professional games costs no more than $10 in Mexico, and you can get the "cheap seats" for a dollar (about 10 **pesos**). Everyone can watch this fun sport on television, too. In Mexico, the sport is played all year round.

Basketball is another team sport in Mexico. In 1936, the Mexican basketball team went to the Olympics and brought back a bronze metal. Basketball is still popular in today's Mexico. Many basketball fans follow America's NBA and choose favorite teams. NBA teams like the San Antonio Spurs have played exhibition games in Mexico. Like other team sports, basketball has

Eduardo Najera plays basketball for the Dallas Mavericks. His game position is power forward. He is the second Mexican-born player ever to be drafted into the NBA. (Manuel Raga, who played during the 1970s, was the first.)

become popular because people can play on the many courts throughout the country, needing just a ball and hoop.

Mexicans also play American football, which they call *futbol Americano*. The popularity of this sport continues growing south of the border, but for many Mexicans, the sport is too expensive. Since football can be a violent **contact sport**, special padded uniforms must be worn to protect against injury. Many Mexican schools cannot afford such equipment, so not every Mexican child can learn to play to this sport. However, even if they cannot play American football themselves, Mexicans are still interested in the sport. Cities like Monterrey, Neuvo León, and Mexico City have hosted pre-season NFL games.

A matador prepares to face down an enraged bull. Once the banderilleros have finished tormenting the animal with sharp sticks, the matador will fight the bull, armed only with a cape and a short sword.

ANIMAL SPORTS
TRADITION OR CRUELTY?

The Spanish term for bullfighting is *corrida de toros*, and the Spaniards were the ones who developed this sport. They brought bullfighting to Mexico when they first arrived in the 1500s. Today, Mexico is home to more than 200 arenas for bullfighting. In fact, the biggest bullring in the world is located in Mexico City. The stadium is called the Plaza de Mexico and holds 50,000 spectators.

As its name suggests, the object of this sport is to fight a bull and survive. The person who attempts this task is called a *matador*. Mexicans treat these bullfighters like stars. Little boys pretend to be these national heroes.

Since an average man may weigh 160 pounds while a bull may weigh over 1,000 pounds, successful matadors must show great

If the crowd thinks a matador gave a wonderful show then the president of the bullring can award the bullfighter with the bull's ears or tail. One ear is cut off and given for a great show. Two ears are given for a grand performance. But for an unforgettable event, two ears and a tail are awarded to the matador.

intelligence and bravery inside the ring. Being a matador is dangerous: one in four is crippled, and one in ten is killed during a bullfight. When bulls become enraged they may gore the bullfighter with their horns. On average, each matador gets gored about once during a six-month season.

Despite the danger he faces, the matador takes great pride in dressing for the big event. He wears an ornate costume called a *traje de luces*. This "suit of lights" can cost thousands of dollars. It consists mainly of a jacket, tight pants, vest, and a hat—all very fancy. They may have silver and gold accents all over for full effect. The outfit's final touch is the crimson red cape. This cape is sometimes draped over the matador's shoulders at the start of the performance. Later, the cape can be waved around to annoy the bulls.

These enormous creatures are not regular cattle. They are *toros de lidia*, fighting bulls bred specifically for bullfighting. Through the years, these bulls have developed a natural tendency to charge. They are more hostile than ordinary bulls.

Most Mexican bullfights take place on Sunday afternoons. Shows may have as many as six bulls lined up for fights. The event begins with rhythmic music playing throughout the stands. Dancing and parades are common too. A greased pig chase or a **rodeo** can be added for the audience's enjoyment. Once these festivities cease, the ground is cleared for the main event.

A bull is set free from his *toril* or pen. He usually arrives in the arena

Bulls do not get mad at the color red. They are actually color-blind. What enrages bulls are moving objects. So they charge at the cape because it moves, not because it is red.

A matador's cape is an essential dramatic element of the sport. More of a psychological threat than a physical one, the matador uses it to excite the bull as well as the crowd.

angry. A beginning matador waves his cape around to excite the bull. Now comes a *picador*. This person rides a horse into the ring. He wears a beige hat called a *castoreno*. He also wears knight-like armor on his legs for protection. He carries at least one lance called a *pica* or *vara*. This lance has a steel point to spear the bull's neck and shoulder area. The maneuver makes the bull lower his head to anticipate the kill. After the bull is lanced, come the *banderilleros*.

The banderilleros, usually three, run up to the bull. They carry brightly colored, sharp sticks called *banderillas*. They poke these sticks into the bull's back. After charging the picador's horse, a bull can be tired, and the banderilleros' job is to enliven it for the final part of the bullfight. The bull may now have been viciously stabbed up to six times. When he is in agonizing pain, he finally meets the real matador.

A bullfighter has only a few minutes of fame: he must kill the bull within 10 minutes of his entrance. His first maneuver is to add to the bull's fury by waving the red cape. The bull charges the matador, and the matador uses catlike movements to escape the sharp horns. The footwork of the bullfighter may be quite graceful and look like a dance with death. After several passes, the matador prepares for the kill. He takes out his sword, called an *estoque*.

The ears and tail of the vanquished bull are often used as symbolic trophies to honor the bravery of the matador. A young bullfighter holds up a bull's ear to the audience.

The matador approaches the exhausted bull. The creature's head is bent down as it submits to the inevitable. The bullfighter thrusts his sword in between the bull's shoulder blades. This move is called the *estocada*. If the bull is still standing, another blade called a *descabello* is used. This sword cuts the spinal cord in the bull's neck. Once the bull is on the ground, a banderillero will spear the bull one last time with a *puntilla*, a small knife. This action signals the end of the bullfight. Onlookers shout *"Olé!"* when they like a move or when the bull is killed.

If the crowd feels that the bull was especially brave, they cheer for the president of the bullring to let the bull take a *vuelta*, a circle around the arena. A *vuelta* makes the bull's breeder very proud and honored. Horses drag the dead bull around the ring to the sound of applause. Finally, the bull's body is pulled out of the arena by the horses. Butchers then cut up the animal and sell the beef.

Can a bull ever enter a bullring and live to tell about it? In rare instances, yes. If a bull has shown exceptional bravery and the crowd petitions the president of the bullring before it is killed, the president will grant an *indulto* (pardon) and spare the bull's life. The matador then pretends to kill the bull with a banderilla. Bulls who are spared usually go on to become **stud** bulls.

Many Mexicans also delight in rooster fights. This "sport" is called cockfighting or *palenque*, and the Spaniards were the ones who brought this form of entertainment to Mexico. During a cockfight, people sit around a dirt pit and place bets. Spectators guess which bird will die first. Cockfighting can bring in many pesos for winning owners.

One bird stands victorious at the end of the cockfight, another popular animal sport across Mexico. Animal rights-supporters have questioned the ethics of a tradition that calls for two birds to fight to the death for entertainment purposes.

To prepare for the fight, handlers tie metal spurs to one leg of each bird. Two roosters are put into the pit. The birds lunge and peck at one another, and the spurs can cause vicious wounds. If one of the birds grows weak, the other may peck at its head. If a time out is called, the handlers hit the birds to get their attention or they may enrage the roosters by plucking their feathers. By the time the birds are back in the ring again, they are furious. When beaks and claws attack, only one bird will live.

Sports like these may seem cruel and bloody to Americans, but they are a part of the Mexican culture. Many Mexicans agree that the sport of bullfighting is rich in culture and high in drama. Some see it as an art form that brings honor to both the country and the matadors. But more and more people are becoming disgusted with the barbaric cruelty of bullfighting. The sport takes place to bring in money from advertising sales, tickets, and beef, but those who oppose bullfighting say that the profits do not justify the sport's cruelty. The bull is not given a chance, so it is not really a bull "fight" but merely a bull death.

Many prominent bullfighters report that the bull is intentionally debilitated with **tranquilizers** and **laxatives**, beatings to the kidneys, petroleum jelly rubbed into their eyes to blur vision, heavy weights hung around their neck for weeks before the fight, and confinement in darkness hours before being released into the bright arena. Some believe that the bull is often still conscious while his ears and tail are cut off. Bulls are usually stabbed several times in the lungs, because the matador frequently misses the heart. Baby bullfights, or *novilladas* are even worse; no matador enters this arena, but instead, spectators stab a calf to death.

An anti-bullfight campaign has been developed to help promote humanity in kids. The campaign has a mascot—Pepe the bull. A person wears this make-believe bull costume when they go into schools. Pepe tries to educate students about animal cruelty.

Fernando Platas of Mexico shows the silver medal he won for diving during the 2000 Olympics. The victory demonstrates the skill that many Mexicans have in water sports.

MEXICO:

WHERE WATER RUNS HIGH
AND ADVENTURE RUNS EVERYWHERE

Thousands of miles of coastlands plus rivers and lakes make Mexico one big water park. The country's mountains and canyons are great ground for backpacking. Ocean waves attract surfers and body boarders. People can look at fish as they snorkel or scuba dive. Or they can catch fish in one of the many seas or lakes. Swimming is a popular activity too.

Many Mexicans enjoy the thrill of surfing. This water sport is especially popular on the west side of the country, the part of Mexico that borders the Pacific Ocean. The areas to surf are plenty, including Boca de Pascuales, Michoacán, and Playa Linda. Boca de Pascuales is a surfer's dream—or nightmare; it's a rivermouth beach that has some of the biggest and fastest waves in Mexico.

Jorge Campos is a famous Mexican goalie from Aculpulco, but while he was growing up, he enjoyed surfing. When he began creating his own soccer outfits, his experiences surfing in Acapulco influenced his choice of bright colors.

31

FERNANDO FABRICIO PLATAS ALVAREZ GETS MEXICO ON BOARD FOR MEDALS

Champions from all over the world competed in the 2000 Olympic games held in Sydney, Australia. On September 26, a Mexican, Fernando Platas, made Olympic history. He took home the silver medal in the three-meter springboard competition. This was Mexico's first silver medal in springboard diving since 1980.

Platas had competed in the 1992 Olympics in Barcelona, Spain, but he had injured his wrist, and he came in 17th in the springboard competition. In the 1996 games in Atlanta, Platas made the final cuts in both springboard and platform diving, coming in seventh and eighth in these events. By the 2000 Olympics, however, he was at the top of his form.

Born on March 16, 1973, Platas is from Mexico City. Growing up, he enjoyed other water sports like swimming and water polo. He also played

land sports like soccer and basketball. Platas looked up to Mexican Olympic divers before him—Joaquin Capilla Perez and Jesús Mena. Perez taught Platas that relaxation is a key element for divers. Perez told Platas that when he dove he used to think about one thing: landing in the water.

The most well known beaches for catching a wave are at Zicatela Beach in Puerto Escondido. This surfing spot hosts so many great waves that it is called the Mexican Pipeline. It is ranked as one of the top surfing destinations in the world. Mexican and other surfers participate in competitions held there each year. Contests may include the Mexpipe August Open, the Longboard Invitational, and the International Surfing Tournament. These events are usually held in the mid- to late summer and early fall.

Many miles of shorelines and lagoons invite swimming. But inland Mexicans may be landlocked, far from lakes and rivers. Since much of Mexico struggles with poverty, pools may be hard to find outside bigger cities. However, many Mexicans practice this sport. Some compete in **meets** from the regional to international levels.

The beauty beneath the sea beckons divers, and snorkeling and scuba diving interest coastal residents of Mexico. Palancar Reef off Cozumel features a collection of coral in a horseshoe formation. Parrot, angle, and butterfly fish come in outrageous colors that delight any diver. The Sea of Cortez offers a chance to swim with whale sharks. Divers can also go to Guerrero Negro's grey whale park. From January to early March, they can watch the California grey whales before they migrate.

Mexico's fishing industry is an important part of the nation's economy, but what is born of necessity can turn into fun. For some, fishing offers a relaxing time to get back to nature. For

In Acapulco, tourists come from across the globe to see the cliff divers. These clavadistas perform for crowds at La Quebrada. They dive from cliffs as high as 1,485 feet (45 meters) into a rough sea.

A windsurfer glides across the sparkling water of Cabo San Lucas. Mexico's water sports are challenging, fun, and scenic.

others, fishing can be a wild adventure. Deep-sea fishing can bring in a wide array of fish, depending on where it is done. The Yucatán Peninsula boasts bonefish, tarpon, snook, jacks, and barracuda. Just off the Baja Peninsula, fisherman can catch blue marlin, dorado, sailfish, tuna, amber jack, or even giant squid.

The adventure sports of Mexico get many hearts pumping. Some popular ways to get an adrenaline rush include kayaking and whitewater rafting. Rivers like Río Filos, Río Bobos, and Río Antigua combine beauty with excitement. The country's hills and mountains also entice **rappelers**

A scuba diver examines the undersea plant life in Cancún. Mexico has become a popular tourist spot in recent years, due in part to scuba diving and other recreational sports.

and mountain climbers alike. Backpacking and camping are a way for nature lovers to catch a glimpse of the wild Mexico, which may be hidden from plain view.

Mexico has nearly 60 national parks and biosphere reserves. These offer everything from volcanoes to caverns, beaches to forests, abundant wildlife to blistering deserts. Because of the land's rich variety, Mexico is a wonderful place to explore—whether by land or water.

A determined cowboy does his best to stay on a bucking bronco at a rodeo. Rodeo animals are often poked and prodded to make them more aggressive, and therefore challenging to control.

MEXICANS RIDE 'EM, ROPE 'EM, AND WRANGLE 'EM

Mexicans sometimes refer to their version of the rodeo—the *charreria*—as their only national sport. This activity is so popular that participants are mentioned in the national anthem of Mexico. *Charros*—a type of cowboys—also participate in local parades, and each year they hold a place of honor in the country's September 16 Independence Day parade. Mexico even appointed a special day to honor the sport. September 14 is Charro Day.

This popular activity goes all the way back to the 1500s. The **conquistadors** of Spain created many of the events of today's Mexican rodeo. These Europeans also brought a main attraction of the

Ever heard the line "get along little dogie"? Cowboys called a calf with no mother a dogie. The term came from the Spanish word *dogal*, meaning a short rope used to keep a calf away from its mother while she was being milked.

37

rodeo—the horse. Native Americans had never even seen a horse or cow until the Spaniards arrived.

Rodeos in Mexico started in Los Llanos de Apan, Hidalgo, where catching bulls by the tail was begun as a sport by Mexican cowboys called *vaqueros*. Shows involving horses and livestock had become well known by the 1800s. Whenever ranchers branded their cattle or rounded them up, they turned the events into great fun. People began traveling long distances to participate or watch the cowboys do their work. Contests developed, and charros would compete to see who handled the livestock the best. Large **fiestas** allowed the cowboys to display their great skill.

With the onset of the Mexican Revolution, many of the large **haciendas** were split up. To keep the charreria tradition alive, charros met in Mexico City. On July 4, 1921, the Asociación Nacional de Charros was born. This association made the rodeo a national sport of Mexico. And in 1933, the Federación Nacional de Charros was founded. This agency set the rules for regional charro groups. The federation gives the okay to people who want to host or participate in Mexican rodeos.

During the 1920s the charreria began changing, so that it was no longer simply a rodeo. Although rodeos and charreria are similar, a few major differences now exist between these two activities. Rodeo is an individual sport—that is to say each contestant competes separately in the events. In charreria, however, teams compete against each other. Another

Mestizos are people who have both American Indian and European backgrounds. Such native peoples and mestizos were the first real cowboys or *vaqueros*.

Horsemen in sombreros look on as a cowboy tries to wrestle a bull to the ground during the mid-1960s. Steeped in the traditions of the 19th century, the rodeo remains a popular form of entertainment in Mexico today.

difference is that people who compete in a rodeo can earn cash prizes, while charros do not earn money if they win events. They compete simply for the honor of their country and the sport.

Many charros grow up around the charreria lifestyle. As children, they often lived on ranches and followed in the bootsteps of their family members. They are often passionate about their vocation, since it is a family tradition handed down from generation to generation.

A Mexican charro rides a bull to demonstrate his talent to onlookers. This level of control requires both experience and bravery to overpower the animal.

Music played by a **mariachi** band usually marks the beginning of the charreria. Members of horseman groups tend to march in front of the crowd first. The state charro association president comes out next. Then team members of opposing teams appear. Some of these people walk, ride horses, or wave banners in support of the sport. After this mini-parade, the competition begins.

Women can participate in charrerias too. They can ride in the escaramunza event, which was begun in the 1950s.

Similar to the American rodeo, the charerria has a series of separate events that determine the overall winner. Scores are given based on how well the horse responds to the rider's orders. Competitors are judged for style as well as execution. The *cala de caballo* involves a horse and rider. The charro must make the horse follow a specific course that may include many twists and turns. The horse even has to be led backward. This event measures the handler's skill as well as the horse's training. Next comes the *pinales al lienzo* (lassos in the curtain). The object is to rope a horse's or bull's hind legs as it gallops past. The *coleadero* is the third part of the sport. The successful entrant rides a horse alongside a bull. He must then pull the bull's tail while turning quickly. This action is supposed to make the bull do a somersault and land on its back. *Jineteo de toros* is bullback riding, while *jineteo de equinos* is horseback riding. In both events, the charro rides the animal until it stops trying to knock him off. *La terna* is next, requiring that a calf be lassoed. The winners are the team who ropes the animal the fastest. Contestants then ride half-wild horses, called broncos. The *piales* and *manganas* require that horsemen rope all four of a horse's legs to make it stop running. The final contest is called the *paso de la muerte*—the death pass. A horseback rider must jump on top of a bronco. He is not to get off the horse until the bucking stops.

Like the bullfight, the charerria is a unique part of Mexican culture.

The fast-paced sport jai alai is intense for players and audience alike. Jai alai requires quick reflexes and great concentration to play.

MEXICANS HOLD THE BALL IN THEIR COURT:

HANDBALL, TENNIS, AND JAI ALAI

Sports that revolve around balls were played by ancient Mexicans. The balls they played with were called *pelotas*, and they were made of rubber, a material not available in Europe. When the Spaniards came to the New World, they had never seen anything like rubber. They were fascinated with it. Over time, Europeans added the native games to their own culture—and they developed new sports that took advantage of this bouncy material.

One of the ancient games was handball, a sport Mexicans still enjoy today. Throughout the country, Mexicans play different variations of their ancestors' sport. In some areas like Oaxaca and Sinaloa, no courts are

Aztecs built their main ball court, called a *tlachco*, in a sacred area. This place was in the middle of Tenochtitlán, their capital city.

These are the ruins of an ancient handball court at Yagul, in Oxaca, Mexico. Spectators would sit on the sloped, stone-faced sides to watch the games.

needed, and people play handball in open spaces. The Chichimeca people were some of the first people to play handball using only one wall. Now, some Mexicans still participate in one-wall handball.

For team handball players, the object of the game is to score the most goals. Players use their hands to make the ball go into the goal. The ball must remain in motion, so people dribble the ball, like in basketball. Any part of the body above the knee can be used to score goals, but kicking the ball is reserved for *goalies* alone. Goals can be quite large, ranging from about six to eight feet high and as wide as 24 feet.

A game that's similar to handball is jai alai. This sport is considered to be the fastest ballgame because the ball is hurled through air at speeds of 188 miles per hour. The game began four centuries ago simply by throwing a ball against a church wall, an activity that was

CIVILIZATIONS OF THE PAST HAD GLORY DAYS TOO

In Mexico, Aztec, Mayan, and Olmec Indians played similar versions of their unique brand of handball long before the Europeans came. We know this because statues from this time period show men playing sports. Some figures look like today's baseball umpires, as they are clad with masks and padding.

An ancestor of handball probably comes from the ancient Maya. The game they played was *pok-a-tok*, a combination of soccer, basketball, racquetball, and volleyball. Players wore padded clothing to prevent injuries. Many wore headpieces like those of warriors and hunters. The main object of the game was to get the ball in a stone hoop. These could be nearly three times as tall as today's basketball hoops! Players also had to keep the ball moving...without using their hands. The Aztecs played a similar game called *tlachtli*.

The games played by these Native Americans did not follow the rules of today's friendly competitions. Instead, a game could be played by feuding regions to avoid war. Many times this handball-like sport became a ritual that crowds came to watch. Losing teams were often sacrificed. Mayan lords took the severed heads of sacrificial victims and bounced them down temple staircases as if they were balls.

first developed in Spain's Basque region. People came to celebrations in this area to see jai alai games. Translated from the Basque word, jai alai means "merry festival." When the Spaniards came to Mexico, they found the natives there already playing their own form of handball, and today's jai alai soon evolved.

Mexicans played jai alai years before a court was built just for the sport, but in 1928, doors opened to Mexico's first jai alai court, built in Mexico City. Now cities like Acapulco, Tijuana, and Cancún have jai alai facilities. Both Mexicans and tourists come to see the exciting sport.

The game's unique equipment sets jai alai apart from any other sport. In other games, substitutions can be made when an item is missing, but this would not work in jai alai. For example, if a goal is missing from a soccer field it can be replaced with some wire and netting. But in jai alai, the tools are very special and hard to replicate. Necessary tools include:

* The ball, or *pelota*. No other sport uses a harder ball. It is a little smaller than a baseball and harder than a baseball bat. Inside the ball is a pure form of Brazilian rubber. Nylon coats this rubber. The outside of the ball is made of goatskin. Balls tend to have short life spans because of the force of the game. Goatskin wraps may come apart just 20 minutes after the start of a game. So extra balls are needed for continued play.

> Mexico is home to the world's oldest known ball court. This court is in Chiapas and is called Paso de la Amada.

* The basket, called the *cesta*. This piece of equipment is essential to the game of jai alai. Players strap this hand-shaped basket to their wrists so they can throw the ball and catch it. The cesta is made of wicker. Players are often measured so their cestas can be handmade just for them. The wicker basket is made from reeds found exclusively in the Pyrenees Mountains, and the frame is made of steam-bent chestnut.

* The court, called the *cancha*. This is no ordinary racquetball court. The driving force and impact of the pelota could crumble regular walls, so builders make the cancha's three walls out of **granite**. Even the mighty pelota cannot tear down these strong walls of rock. The court's size can vary, but if you cut a football field in half, then built 40-foot walls on three sides and see-through wiring on the fourth side, you'd have something about the size of most canchas.

Handball is another intense game that has caught on in Mexico and around the world. The game necessitates great mental and physical control.

Most of the time, eight teams play jai alai. Every time a team bounces the ball out of bounds or fails to catch the ball in the cesta, the other team scores a point. If a team cannot catch the ball after only one bounce, then the other team also gains a point. If a player does not return the ball fast enough, the other team again gets a point. In round one, the first team plays the second team. Whoever wins this match plays the third team. The losing team stands at the back of the line for their next turn to play. The point value jumps to two when the second round begins. In most games, the team who earns seven points first is declared the winner.

The object of jai alai is to hurl a ball against the front wall as close to the side wall of the court with so much speed and spin that the opposition cannot catch or return it on the fly or the first bounce. Like tennis, the game starts with a serve. The ball can only bounce one time on the floor before being caught. The teams continue catching the ball and throwing it back to one another, and the ball must remain in motion. Judges keep constant watch to see if a player fails to catch the ball or throws it out of bounds.

Due to the fast-paced and dangerous nature of the game, jai alai can be tough. It can take years of training and practice to succeed in the sport. But couch potatoes can enjoy this exciting sport too. Many canchas are built for spectators who come to watch and wager. Gamblers can win money guessing which team will come in first or second.

The ball court located in the ancient city of Chichén Itzá is the largest court ever uncovered. This court is the size of a modern soccer field. It is located near Cancún in the Yucatán Peninsula.

Cestas, the woven glove-baskets used to play jai alai, are made in workshops like this. Making the cesta is an intricate process, and these workers can only turn out five a day.

Although tennis seems far tamer by comparison, this sport also continues to gain fans in Mexico. While most people watch rather than play, tennis courts can be found in different parts of the country. Tournaments like the Mexican Tennis Open draw international attention. But the equipment and training needed to play can be expensive. For this reason, not every Mexican can afford what it takes to become a true tennis enthusiast.

MEXICANS SALUTE SOLO SPORTS

Sports in which individuals compete are popular in Mexico. Track and field activities like running and racewalking interest many people. Lifting weights is another way to work out alone, and Mexicans are also discovering the advantages of golf. Ring sports like boxing are found throughout the countryside and draw many crowds. Cycling both on tracks and off-road terrain make bicycles a common choice for sports fans.

Jogging and running are of interest to many Mexicans. Both cross-country running and sprinting offer a challenging workout. The natural beauty of Mexico's coastlines, mountains, and canyons make even the most routine run refreshing for body, mind, and soul. Mexican track meets and races are not common, however. Many Mexican runners practice in their homeland but enter international events. Runners like

Runner Ana Guevara celebrates a well-run race at the World Championships in Athletics in 2001. Both long-distance and sprint running have been popular in Mexico for centuries.

Alejandro Cardenas shows the bronze medal for the 400 meter sprint which he earned at the Olympic Games in 2000.

Ana Guevara, Adriana Fernandez, and Alejandro Cardeas represented Mexico in the Sydney Olympics in 2000.

The marathon demands that entrants be in great shape. This event consists of running 26.2 miles. German Silva finished a respectable fifth place in the 1996 Olympics. To train for such a run, he and other top Mexican runners train at Nevado de Toluca, where the volcano called Xinantecatl churns out champions. This Mexican landmark towers at 15,387 feet (4,663 meters). At the top, temperatures are well below freezing. At the base, desert-like conditions make the air scorchingly hot. Because it requires more effort to breathe, running at such high altitudes strengthens lungs, while the high temperatures at the volcano's base help build endurance. While he was training, Silva lived in a hostel at 12,300 feet. He conditioned his body by making it

SORAYA JIMENEZ MENDOVIL

Mexicans will never forget the 2000 Olympics in Sydney, Australia. On September 18, an unforgettable event occurred: Soraya Jimenez became the first woman to ever win a gold medal for Mexico. She earned the only gold medal ever won for weightlifting in her country. This was the first gold medal for Mexico since the 1984 games in Los Angeles, and Jimenez was the first woman to ever win a medal in weightlifting for Mexico.

Jimenez became a leading Latina when she won the 58-kilogram weightlifting category. The 23-year-old measures only five feet tall and weighs in at 128 pounds—but the stocky athlete lifted an amazing 281 pounds for the win. How could she manage such a feat? "All I can say is practice," Jimenez said. "You never know what you might do." The Mexican Olympian is a law school student from a Mexico City suburb. In her spare time she enjoys basketball and badminton.

Her victory in Sydney continues to inspire young women in Mexico. President Fox said, "This medal gives us back our self-confidence and makes us feel that we're capable of doing anything, that we can win."

A native Mexican runs in a footrace that is part of the Feast of San Lorenzo celebration. Running is viewed by Mexican tribes not only as exercise but as recreation also.

adjust to such a change in altitude. His shelter did not even have heat, water, or electricity. He traded showers and hot meals for the sheer love of running.

Running is nothing new for a breed of Mexicans called the Tarahumaras. Their real name is Raramuri, which means "the people who are light of foot." They are probably the purest Indians that still exist in Mexico. The Tarahumaras consider running part of their civilization. These people practice their basic belief of living in harmony with both nature and neighbors. Today, many still wear traditional clothing. Men wear loincloths and baggy cotton shirts. Women wear skirts and a loosely fitted cotton blouses. And everyone wears headbands.

In earlier times, the Tarahumaras ran long distances through the countryside. But new developments and construction have forced them into a remote area. They now live in the Sierra Tarahumara, an area of Chihuahua high above sea level. Through the years, their lungs have adjusted to the high altitude and become stronger because of it. This added lungpower makes these runners hard to beat.

Tarahumaras love to eat and run. They created their own version of fast food years ago when they ran so swiftly they would actually chase down their dinner! Deer and mountain goats could not outrun them. Today, Tarahumaras run relays without stopping. Some of these races can exceed 230 miles.

At the 2000 Olympics in Sydney, the world could not deny that Mexico produces great racewalkers. Noe Hernandez Valentin won the silver medal in the 20-kilometer event. Joel Sanchez Guerrero brought home the bronze in the 50-kilometer event.

For nearly 20 years, Julio Cesar Chavez dominated the welterweight boxing class. He recently retired with a record of 103–5–2, including 86 wins by knockout.

Bicycling is another recreation Mexicans enjoy, but in some areas of Mexico, bicycles are not seen as sports equipment but as transportation. In bigger cities, people use bicycles to get around town and avoid traffic. But recreational cycling draws Mexican fans. In more populated areas, like Mexico City, cyclists can use tracks. Mountain bikers can explore Mexico's majestic backcountry. Chihuahua's colorful

Copper Canyon and the great, green gorges of the Sierra Madre mountains offer cyclists adventure. Every year, cyclists can compete in a variety of tournaments sponsored in Mexico.

Individual contact sports are also popular in Mexico. Several top boxers have come from Mexico, including Julio Cesar Chavez. Cities may host boxing tournaments, but even in remote areas, villagers practice their boxing techniques. Some of these events may be in fields and can draw a crowd. Mexicans call wrestling *luche libre*, or free fight. Spectators can buy tickets to watch this form of international wrestling.

Golfing appeals to Mexicans who enjoy solo sports, and golfers are finding more and more areas to play throughout the country. Guadalajara is considered the golf capital of Mexico. This city has about six different courses that are nice enough for champions to putt on. Golf used to be just for the very rich, but as more courses are built and the sport gains more fans, greater numbers of Mexicans have the opportunity to tee off.

Up until the year 2000, no Mexican ever received an Olympic medal in martial arts. But Victor Manuel Estrada Garibay changed that. He was the first Mexican to bring home an Olympic medal in tae kwon do. Estrada won the bronze medal in the 80-kilogram category at the Sydney Olympics.

Whether their games are ancient or new, solo or team, Mexicans love to play. In short, the sports of Mexico are as diverse as the country itself.

CHRONOLOGY

1000-400 B.C.	The Olmec civilization thrives in Mexico; it plays some form of ballgame.
300-900 A.D.	The Maya, also ballplayers, dominate the Yucatán Peninsula. The Aztecs rule central Mexico; they play a form of basketball.
1800s	Soccer is introduced in Mexico; rodeos become popular.
1890s	Baseball grows in popularity in Mexico.
1902	The first amateur soccer league begins with five teams.
1910	The Mexican Revolution begins.
1921	With the end of the Mexican Revolution, baseball spreads throughout Mexico; the Asociación Nacional de Charros is formed.
1928	Mexico's first jai alai court opens in Mexico City.
1929	Mexico joins the Federation Internationale de Football Association (FIFA).
1930	Mexico plays in the first FIFA World Cup game.
1933	Federacion Nacional de Charros is developed to regulate charro groups.
1936	Mexico's basketball team takes the bronze medal at the Olympic games.
1948	Horseback riders win Mexico's first Olympic gold medals. The historic events were individual and team showjumping.
1955	The Mexican League of baseball is formed.
1960	The Mexican Central League is formed.

1968 Two boxers win gold medals at the Olympics: Antonio Roldan wins in the featherweight category and Ricardo Delgado wins in the flyweight.

1970 Manuel Raga becomes the first Mexican-born player to be drafted by the NBA; he plays for the Hawks; Mexico hosts the World Cup finals.

1984 Jose Manuel Youshimatz wins Mexico's only Olympic medal in cycling; he takes the bronze in the 50-kilometer race.

1986 Jorge Campos signs on with UNAM (Pumas); Mexico again hosts the World Cup finals.

1992 Vinny Castilla is drafted by the Colorado Rockies.

1994 Mexico plays in the USA World Cup.

1995 The first Mexican National One-Wall Championships are held in Guadalupe.

1996 Pepe the bull becomes active in Mexico City's anti-bullfight campaign.

1998 Mexico plays in the France World Cup.

1999 Adriana Fernandez wins the New York City Marathon; she is the first woman of Mexico to accomplish this feat.

2000 Soraya Jimenez lifts her way to the gold medal podium at the Sydney Olympics.

2002 The Mexican *futbol* team plays in the World Cup.

2004 Four Mexican athletes win medals at the Olympic Games in Athens: Ana Guevara (silver, 400m), Belem Guerrero (silver, cycling), Oscar Salazar (silver, Taekwondo), and Iridia Salazar (bronze, Taekwondo).

FURTHER READING

Baddiel, Ivor. *Ultimate Soccer*. New York: DK Publishing, 1998.

Bale, John. *Sports Geography*. New York: E. & F.N. Spon, 1989.

Bale, John and Joseph Maguire. *The Global Sports Arena: Athletic Talent Migration in an Interdependent World*. London: Frank Cass, 1994.

Kalman, Bobbie. *Mexico the Culture*. New York: Crabtree Publishing Company, 1993.

Mood, Dale, Frank Musker, and Judith Rink. *Sports and Recreational Activities for Men and Women*. Chicago: Mosby Year Book, 1991.

Murray, Bill. *The World's Game a History of Soccer*. Chicago: University of Illinois Press, 1996.

Stein, R. Conrad. *Mexico*. New York: Children's Press, 1998.

INTERNET RESOURCES

Charreria
www.tsha.utexas.edu/handbook/online/articles/view/CC/llc4.html

Handball
www.edunetconnect.com/cat/games/handball.html

Bullfight FAQs
www.bullfights.org/faq/index.shtml

The Conquest of Fear—Latino Style
www.mexconnect.com/mex_/bull.html

GLOSSARY

Amateurs	People who engage in sport for recreation rather than pay.
Arena	An enclosed area used for public entertainment.
Conquistadors	The Spanish conquerors of the New World.
Contact sport	A game that involves physical contact between contestants.
Fiestas	Spanish parties or celebrations.
Goalies	The player who guards the goal in soccer to prevent the opposite team from scoring.
Granite	A hard, igneous rock.
Haciendas	Large Mexican estates or plantations.
Laxatives	A drug that loosens bowel movements and may cause diarrhea.
Leagues	Groups of teams that regularly play against each other.
Mariachi	A type of music played by Mexican street bands.
Meets	Competitions.
Pesos	Mexican units of money.
Rappelers	People who descend down a cliff suspended from a rope.
Recruit	To enlist new members for a team.
Rodeo	A public performance that involves bronco riding, calf roping, steer wrestling, and bull riding.
Scouts	People who look for new talent for sports teams.
Stud	An animal used for breeding young.
Tranquilizers	Drugs used to calm or sedate.
Umpire	The official who sees that the rules are obeyed during a game.

INDEX

PICTURE CREDITS

2	Hulton/Archive	40	Hulton/Archive
3	Hulton/Archive	42	Owen Franken/Corbis
10	Hulton/Archive	44	Macduff Everton/Corbis
12	Hulton/Archive	47	Reuters NewMedia Inc./Corbis
15	Hulton/Archive	49	Hulton/Archive
17	Macduff Everton/Corbis	50	Hulton/Archive
20	Owen Franken/Corbis	52	Hulton/Archive
23	Stephanie Maze/Corbis	53	Hulton/Archive
25	AFP/Corbis	54	Craig Aurness/Corbis
27	Danny Lehman/Corbis	56	Michael Brennan/Corbis
30	Hulton/Archive		
32	Hulton/Archive	Cover	(front) Danny Lehman/Corbis
34	Corbis Images		(inset) IMS Communications
35	Corbis Images		(back) Macduff Everton/Corbis
36	Adam Woolfitt/Corbis		
39	Hulton/Archive		

CONTRIBUTORS

Roger E. Hernández is the most widely syndicated columnist writing on Hispanic issues in the United States. His weekly column, distributed by King Features, appears in some 40 newspapers across the country, including the *Washington Post*, *Los Angeles Daily News*, *Dallas Morning News*, *Arizona Republic*, *Rocky Mountain News* in Denver, *El Paso Times*, and *Hartford Courant*. He is also the author of *Cubans in America*, an illustrated history of the Cuban presence in what is now the United States, from the early colonists in 16th-century Florida to today's Castro-era exiles. The book was designed to accompany a PBS documentary of the same title.

Hernández's articles and essays have been published in the *New York Times*, *New Jersey Monthly*, *Reader's Digest*, and *Vista Magazine*; he is a frequent guest on television and radio political talk shows, and often travels the country to lecture on his topic of expertise. Currently, he is teaching journalism and English composition at the New Jersey Institute of Technology in Newark, where he holds the position of writer-in-residence. He is also a member of the adjunct faculty at Rutgers University.

Hernández left Cuba with his parents at the age of nine. After living in Spain for a year, the family settled in Union City, New Jersey, where Hernandez grew up. He attended Rutgers University, where he earned a BA in Journalism in 1977; after graduation, he worked in television news before moving to print journalism in 1983. He lives with his wife and two children in Upper Montclair, New Jersey.

Erica M. Stokes is a freelance writer. Her work for children and young adults has been published in magazines, Web sites, software, and books. She currently resides in the Tennessee Valley of northern Alabama.